CONTENTS

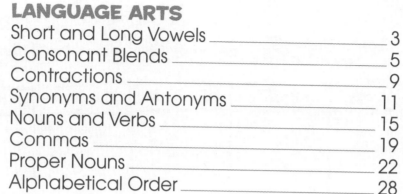

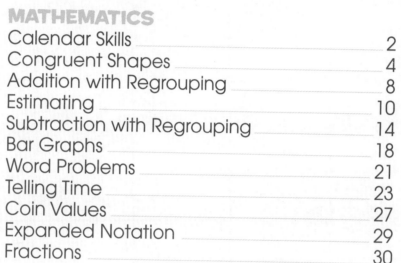
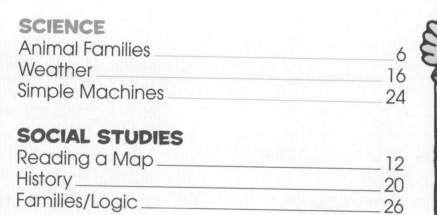
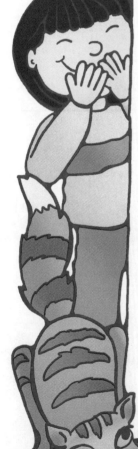

ARKING THE DAYS

Fill in the missing dates. Then mark the calendar with Troy's special days.

Try It! Make a calendar for next month. Mark things that you will do that month.

Sunday	Monday	Tuesday	Wednesday	Thursday	Friday	Saturday
			1	2		
		7		9	10	
12		14	15	16		
	20	21		23		25
26	27				31	

1. Troy's birthday is the third Wednesday. Draw a  on the day.

2. He plays baseball every Monday. Draw a to mark each day.

3. Troy is going to the fair on the fourth Saturday. Mark the day with an **X**.

4. His cousin is visiting on the last Thursday. Draw a on the day.

Did You Know?

The ancient Egyptian calendar had 12 months, each 30 days long. By studying the stars, they learned to add five days to the year to make 365 days.

2

SKATE MIX-UP

Make pairs by finding skates with the same vowel sounds. Draw lines to show the pairs.

Try It! Write a sentence using only long vowel words. Make your sentence at least five words long.

 rain

 best

 flat

 trap

 tree

 sale

 desk

 bead

 cry

 side

 code

 boat

Did You Know?

The first ice skates were animal bones strapped to a person's feet. Skaters had to use a stick to push themselves on the ice!

PUZZLING SHAPES

Congruent figures are exactly the same shape and size.

 and ▲ are congruent. So are ⬟ and ⬠.

Write the number of the congruent shape in the puzzle.

Try It!
Look around. See if you can find things with these shapes.

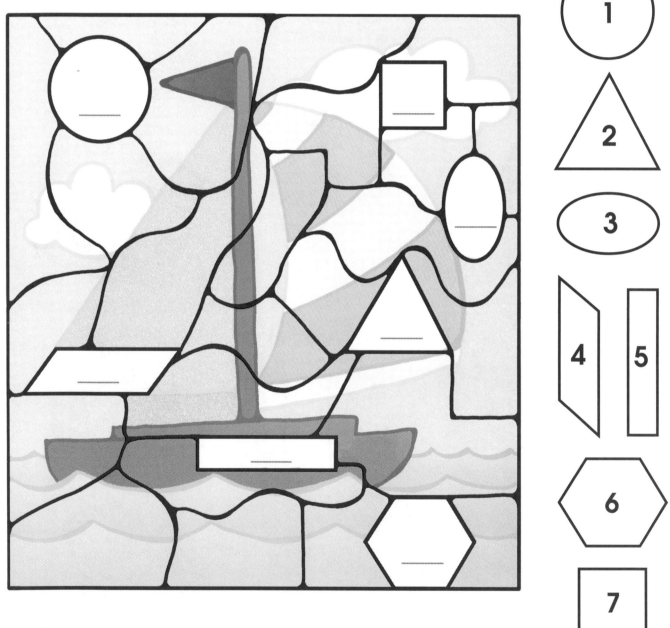

1

2

3

4   5

6

7

 Make a jigsaw puzzle of your own. Draw a picture on heavy paper. Cut it into 10–12 pieces. Give the puzzle to a friend to solve!

4

ZOO BLENDS

A **consonant blend** is two or more consonants that work together. For example, **b** and **l** work together in the word **blue**.

These animal names begin with consonant blends. Add the missing consonants to each animal name.

Try It!
Write a sentence that has four words that start with blends. Here is a start: Twenty swans...

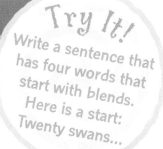

1. ___ ___ ake

2. ___ ___ og

3. ___ ___ unk

4. ___ ___ amingo

5. ___ ___ ocodile

6. ___ ___ an

7. ___ ___ izzly bear

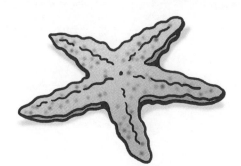

8. ___ ___ arfish

9. ___ ___ ab

Did You Know?

The oldest U.S. zoo is in Central Park in New York City. It opened in 1864.

Try It! Choose an animal family. Cut out pictures of animals from that family and make a collage.

Read each sign. Write the name of the animal family on the box that describes it.

Pete's Perfect Pets

Birds
Reptiles
Insects
Mammals
Fish
Amphibians

1. These animals are furry. They feed their young milk.

2. These animals have scaly skin. Most of them live on land.

Help Pete put the pets where they belong.
Write the number for the animal family above each picture below.

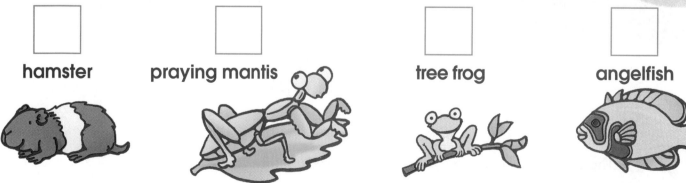

hamster	praying mantis	tree frog	angelfish

The blue whale is the largest living animal. It can be 100 feet long.

These animals have wings. They lay eggs.

3.

These animals live in water when they are young. They have smooth, moist skin.

4.

These animals have six legs. They have three body parts.

5.

These animals live in water. They breathe through gills.

6.

dog

grasshopper

turtle

parrot

Don't let addition bug you!
Add the numbers. Then write the sums.

Try It!
Circle the bug with the least sum. Put an X on the bug with the greatest sum.

Remember!
Sometimes you need to regroup when you add.

$$45$$
$$+26$$
$$71$$

5+6=11
1+4+2=7

E
22
+14

M
49
+ 8

T
14
+40

F
25
+ 7

K
38
+11

L
27
+13

Use your answers to decode the riddle. Write the letter for each answer. Some letters are used more than once.

Where is the best place to buy bugs?

A
16
+ 5

R
42
+36

A ___ ___ ___ ___
  32   40   36   21

___ ___ ___ ___ ___ ___
57   21   78   49   36   54

8

LET'S FLY A KITE!

Try It!
Write a story about flying a kite. Use at least three contractions in your story.

A **contraction** is a short way to write two words.

Read each sentence. Underline two words that can be written as a contraction. Then write the number of each sentence in the kite with that contraction.

1. Some kites will not stop crashing!
2. My kite went so high, I could not see it.
3. One kite is not flying.
4. Father says he is glad we came.
5. I did not know kites were so much fun.
6. I can not wait to come back.
7. I will bring a new kite next time.

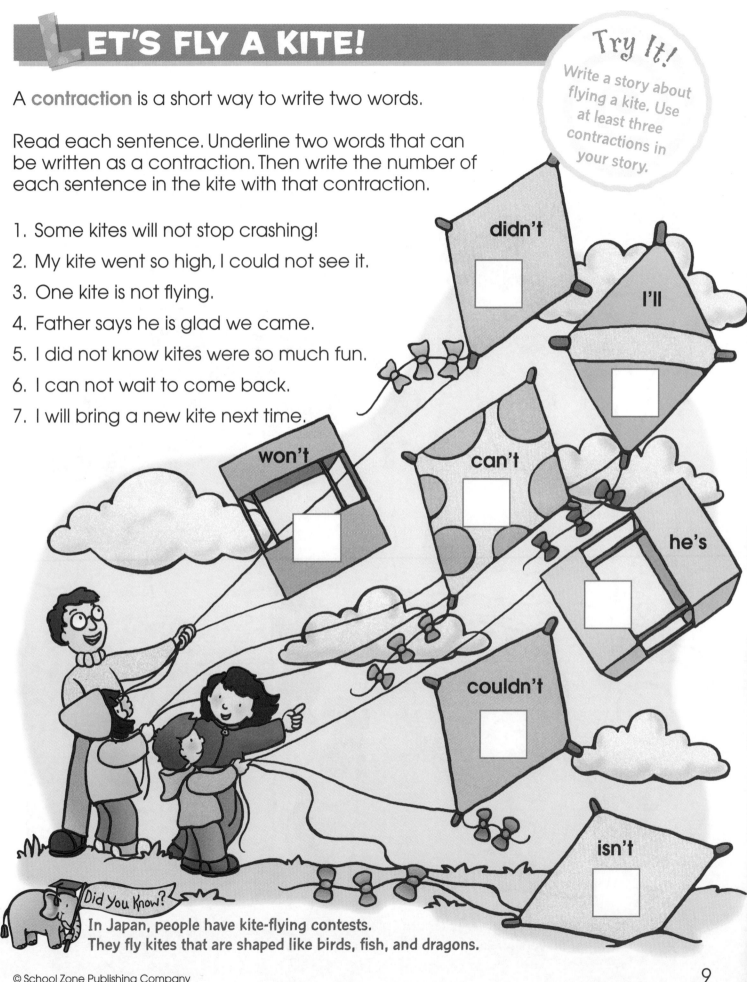

didn't

I'll

won't

can't

he's

couldn't

isn't

Did You Know?
In Japan, people have kite-flying contests. They fly kites that are shaped like birds, fish, and dragons.

9

TAKE A GUESS!

Look at the plates of jelly beans. Don't count! Estimate how many are on each plate. Write your estimate. Then circle groups of five and count. How close were you?

Try It! Write about a time when you had to guess something. How did you feel? Did you guess correctly?

Word to Know
The word **estimate** means to guess.

1. Estimate _____
Number _____

2. Estimate _____
Number _____

3. Estimate _____
Number _____

4. Estimate _____
Number _____

Cool Idea Play an estimation game. Take turns placing small objects on a table. The other players guess how many. Then count. The winner has the closest guess.

SAME OR DIFFERENT

Synonyms are words that mean almost the same thing. **Big** and **large** are synonyms. **Antonyms** are words with opposite meanings. **Big** and **little** are antonyms.

Try It!
Choose one of the words below. List as many synonyms as you can.
little pretty nice

Read the sentences. Write **S** if the bold words are synonyms. Write **A** if they are antonyms. The first one is done for you.

A 1. The ground was **wet** when we got to the farm. By afternoon, it was **dry**.

_____ 2. The **branches** were loaded with apples. Some **limbs** touched the ground.

_____ 3. The farmer said the turkeys were **wild**. But the chickens acted **tame**.

_____ 4. The farmer put the **mound** of hay next to a **pile** of dirt.

_____ 5. Our hands got so **dirty**! It took a lot of soap to get them **clean**.

_____ 6. The farmer sat on a **huge** tractor. He looked **tiny** up there.

_____ 7. We watched the farmer **chop** down a tree. Then he **cut** it into logs.

Cool Idea

Write a story about a trip you have taken. Use some synonyms and antonyms in your writing.

LUCKY LODGE

Try It!
Make up another question that can be answered by studying this map.

Juanita and her family went to Lucky Lodge for a long weekend.

Use the map to answer the questions.

1. Find Silver City. What direction is Lucky Lodge from Silver City?

   north   northeast   northwest

2. Find Frog Pond. What direction is Lake Sycamore from Frog Pond?

   east   north   southwest

Map Key

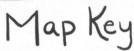 road

 footpath

 town

 forest

 river

 picnic area

Make a map of your bedroom, neighborhood, or classroom. Be sure to include a map key.

Frog Pond

Sycamore

Sunnyville

3. Which picnic area can be reached by road?

Lake Sycamore   Loon Lake   Frog Pond

4. Which town is closest to Lake Sycamore?

Sunnyville   Silver City   Newtown

5. Which cannot be reached by footpath?

Lake Sycamore   a picnic area   Loon Lake

6. Which body of water is closest to Silver City?

Lake Sycamore   Loon Lake   Frog Pond

LOST LUNCHES

Solve the subtraction problems. Then match the number on the food with the answers. Write the food under the correct lunch box or bag.

1. _____

2. _____

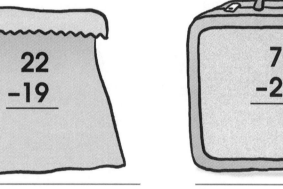

3. _____

4. _____

5. _____

6. _____

Try It!

Plan a menu for your lunch box. Copy it on a fancy piece of paper to make it special.

Remember!

Sometimes you need to regroup when you subtract.

$$\begin{array}{r} {}^{6\ 12} \\ \cancel{7}\cancel{2} \\ -\ 46 \\ \hline 26 \end{array}$$

12−6=6
6−4=2

26 apple	19 pizza
3 milk	52 orange
51 soup	58 juice

14

IT'S PLAYTIME!

Try It!
Write a sentence that has two nouns and one verb. Underline the nouns and circle the verb.

Nouns are naming words. They name people, places, or things.

Circle the nouns.

1. The boys and girls ran on the grass.

2. The swings were wet.

Verbs are action words. They tell what is happening or what someone is doing.

Underline the verbs.

3. The children ran up the hill.

4. Their teacher blew the whistle.

Finish these sentences by writing a noun or a verb. Write **n** if you wrote a noun. Write **v** if you wrote a verb.

5. Three _____ sat on the bench. ☐

6. A boy _____ into the mud. ☐

7. The children went past the _____ . ☐

8. The teacher _____ the ball. ☐

9. A girl _____ on the monkey bars. ☐

Cool Idea Draw a picture that shows you and your friends playing together. Label five nouns by writing a word next to its picture. For example, draw a ball and then write the word ball next to it.

MAP THE WEATHER

Weather forecasters make maps that show what the weather will be like for the day.

Use the key to answer the questions.

Try It!
Make a chart to track the weather. Record the date, temperature, and condition of each day.

1. Which city will have the warmest temperature?

   Portland   Washington D.C.   Dallas

2. Which part of the country will have the coolest temperature?

   south   west   north

3. What will the weather be like in Miami?

   rainy and freezing   sunny and hot   rainy and hot

4. What kind of weather will Denver have?

   sunny and warm   sunny and cold   rainy and hot

5. Which part of the country will have the most rain?

   south   east   north

6. What kind of precipitation is St. Paul going to have?

   rain   snow   hail

Fantastic Cloud Maker

With a little help you can make your own cloud.

1. Ask an adult to fill a jar with hot tap water and then pour out half the water.

2. Cover the jar with plastic wrap. Be careful not to burn your hands on the jar.

3. Place several ice cubes on top of the plastic wrap. You'll see a cloud in the jar!

You Need
• a clear jar
• plastic wrap
• ice
• hot tap water

There are lots of sayings about the weather. Here's one!
Red sky at night, sailor's delight.
Red sky at morning, sailors take warning.

Word to Know
Precipitation is the form in which water comes to the earth. Rain, snow, hail, and sleet are all kinds of precipitation.

Map Key
- ☀ sunshine
- ☁ partly cloudy
- ⛈ thunderstorms
- 🌧 rain
- hail
- ❄ snow

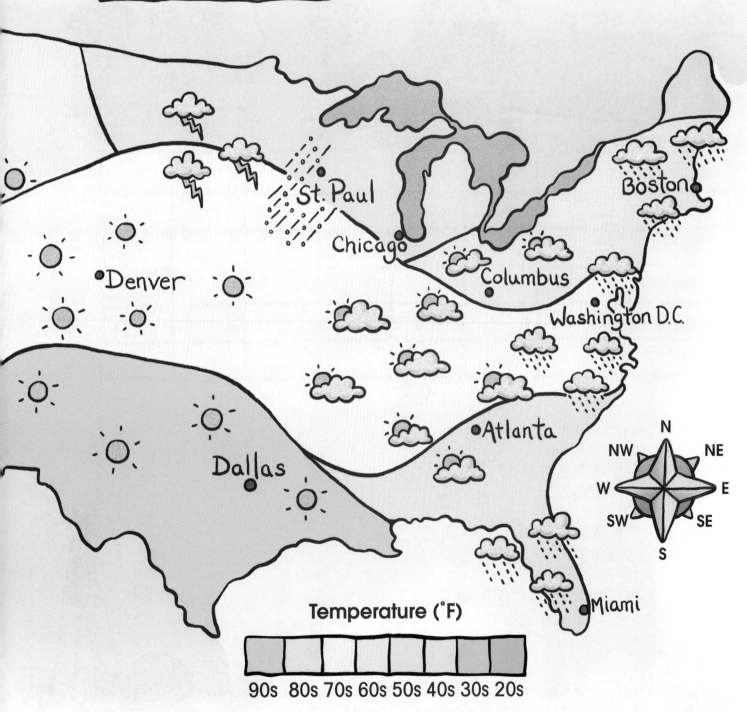

St. Paul

Chicago

Boston

Denver

Columbus

Washington D.C.

Atlanta

Dallas

N
NW   NE
W   E
SW   SE
S

Miami

Temperature (°F)

90s 80s 70s 60s 50s 40s 30s 20s

Try It!
Ask 10 people to name their favorite sport. Make a graph to show their answers.

Tyler asked his friends to name their favorite sports. Use what he learned to finish the graph below.

Favorite Sports

football	IIII
swimming	II
soccer	ЖЖ
baseball	ЖЖ I
running	I
skating	III

	1	2	3	4	5	6	7
football							
swimming							
soccer							
baseball							
running							
skating							

Use the graph.

1. How many more kids like baseball than swimming? _____

2. How many fewer kids like skating than football? _____

3. How many kids in all did Tyler ask to name their favorite sport? _____

Cool Idea

What's your favorite sport? Write two or three sentences telling why you like it. Draw a picture of yourself playing the sport.

18

PET PICNIC

Try It!
Write a sentence about your favorite dinner. Include at least four foods. Use commas in your sentence.

Commas separate items in a list. How do commas make these two sentences different?

Emma called Ryan, Mary Ann, and Tony.
Emma called Ryan, Mary, Ann, and Tony.

The first sentence names *three* friends.
Ryan
Mary Ann
Tony

The second sentence names *four* friends.
Ryan   Ann
Mary   Tony

Answer the question after each sentence.

1. Mary Ann's pets are named Fifi, Rose Marie, and Scamp.

   How many pets does Mary Ann have? _____

2. Emma watched Rose, Marie, Tyrone, and Sunee play ball.

   How many kids played ball? _____

3. Emma brought ice, cream, peanuts, butter, and pizza.

   How many things did Emma bring? _____

4. The pets ate pizza, ice cream, peanut butter, and cookies!

   How many things did the pets eat? _____

5. Mary Ann, Fifi, Rose Marie, and Scamp went home.

   How many people and animals went home? _____

Commas are used in dates, too. A comma separates the day and the year. Put commas where they belong in these dates.

May 10 2002   July 31 2003   September 23 2002

NOW AND THEN

Match the letter of the phrase from the Word Box with each picture. Write **then** if people did it in the past. Write **now** if people do it today.

Try It!
Think of two ways that life is the same today as it was 200 years ago. Write two sentences.

Word Box

a. buy with credit cards
b. send a telegraph
c. use a washing machine
d. trade for things you need
e. hand-wash clothes
f. send an e-mail

a

now

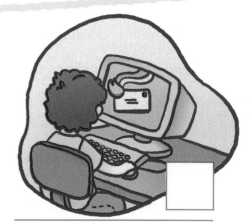

Try living one day like a person in colonial times. Ask your parents to help you bake bread. Play games without computers, and don't watch TV. Write a paragraph to describe what your day was like.

BATTER UP!

Find the answers to the baseball word problems.

Try It! Write a word problem of your own. Then ask someone to solve it. Make sure you know the answer!

Remember! When solving word problems, look for words that give you hints about whether to add or subtract.

1. The Tigers played the Stars.
   Each team had 12 players.
   How many players were there in all? _____

2. Todd hit a ball 112 feet.
   Fred hit a ball 123 feet.
   How many more feet did Fred's ball go? _____

3. There were 77 people in the bleachers.
   There were seats for 85 people.
   How many seats were empty? _____

4. A snack bar hamburger costs $1.25.
   A slice of pizza costs $0.95.
   How much more does a hamburger cost? _____

5. The snack bar sold 52 hot dogs,
   30 hamburgers, and 14 pizza slices.
   How many items were sold in all? _____

Did You Know? In the 1830s, Americans played a game called "town ball." It was like baseball. Wooden stakes or stones were used for bases and the ball was yarn wound around a piece of rubber.

BEST FRIENDS

Proper nouns are nouns that name a certain person, place, or thing. They always start with a capital letter.

Here are some proper nouns.

Bobby	Ms. Jones	New York City
Friday	May	Main Street

Underline the proper nouns in each sentence. Write them correctly on the lines.

Try It!
Write a paragraph about yourself and your friends. Circle all the proper nouns in your paragraph.

1. My best friend will visit on saturday. _____

2. His name is tom lee. _____

3. He lives on south street. _____

4. Tom's birthday is in march. _____

5. We go to parkside school. _____

6. Our teacher is mrs. montez. _____

Cool Idea

Use proper nouns to answer these questions. Who is one of your friends? What is the name of your school? What is your favorite holiday?

Write each animal's name under the clock that shows the time it will see the doctor.

Word to Know
A **veterinarian** is a doctor whose patients are animals. "Vet" is a short way of saying "veterinarian."

1. _____

2. _____

3. _____

4. _____

5. _____

Posey 12:45

Squawk 2:30

Buster 1:30

Fluffy 1:15

Shelley 4:15

ACHINES AT WORK

Machines help us do work. They make work easier.
The six machines below are called **simple machines**.

Try It!
Draw a machine made of two simple machines. What can your machine do?

lever

wheel and axle

wedge

inclined plane

pulley

screw

COOL IDEA!

You can lift pennies without touching them. Balance a ruler on a small block. Put four pennies on one end. Push the other end down. The ruler is a lever to lift the pennies.

Look at the picture. Write the names of the simple machines in the boxes.

25

Try It!
Draw a picture that shows two or more generations of your family.

The picture shows people in Tanya's family. Read the clues. Label each person with the letter next to his or her name.

Clues

1. Tanya likes puppies better than cats.
2. Toni and Tanya are twins.
3. Adam is three years younger than Tanya.
4. Aunt Jan wears glasses.
5. Uncle Joe has a beard.
6. Uncle Ryan wears a hat.

Tanya's Family

a. Aunt Casey
b. Tanya
c. Aunt Jan
d. Uncle Ryan
e. Adam
f. Toni
g. Uncle Joe

Try It!

If you buy the ball with a dollar bill, how much change will you get back?

There are lots of toys at this yard sale! Circle the coins you need to buy the toy. Use the fewest coins you can.

 quarter = 25¢   dime = 10¢    nickel = 5¢   penny = 1¢

1.

2.

3.

4.

Did You Know?

U.S. coins are made in two different places. Look at a coin. If you see a tiny **D**, it was made in Denver, Colorado. If you see a **P**, it was made in Philadelphia, Pennsylvania.

ABC order is the order of the letters in the alphabet. These words are in ABC order.

    ant   blue   ding

When words start with the same letter, use the second letter to put them in ABC order.

    pig   plant   pumpkin

Look at the sets of books. Use the **author's last name** to number them 1, 2, 3, and 4 in ABC order. The first set is done for you.

1.

Snake Hunt by H.S. Fang — **3**

Cub Kitchen by Ted E. Bear — **1**

Cats and Dogs by Red Setter — **4**

Bee Attack! by Hy Bumble — **2**

2.

Racing for Fun by Howie Fast

Swimming Tips by Lee Lake

Home Run! by Ima Hitter

Gymnastics by Flip N. Jump

3.

Mountain Trail by Oma Blisters

Jungle Trek by Annie Body

Oceans Away by C. Breeze

Desert Heat by Sandy Beach

Try It! Find five books. Put them in ABC order by the author's last name.

28

STRETCHED NUMBERS

Try It!
You can stretch large numbers, too!
1,402 = 1,000 + 400 + 2
Try one of your own!

To understand large numbers, try stretching them out.

238 = 2 hundreds + 3 tens + 8 ones
238 = 200 + 30 + 8

Stretch these numbers.

1. 436 = ____ hundreds + ____ tens + ____ ones

   436 = _____ + _____ + _____

2. 613 = ____ hundreds + ____ tens + ____ ones

   613 = _____ + _____ + _____

3. 804 = ____ hundreds + ____ tens + ____ ones

   804 = _____ + _____ + _____

4. 277 = ____ hundreds + ____ tens + ____ ones

   277 = _____ + _____ + _____

5. 480 = ____ hundreds + ____ tens + ____ ones

   480 = _____ + _____ + _____

Cool Idea

Ask someone to measure your height. Then measure your stretched-out arms. How do the measurements compare?

Look at each pizza. Write the fraction that tells how much of the pizza was eaten.

Try It!
Draw two identical pizzas. Show that one has 2/4 left. The other has 1/2 left. Compare the pizzas.

Word to Know!

The top number in a fraction is called the **numerator**. The bottom number in a fraction is called the **denominator**.

numerator

$$\frac{3}{10}$$

denominator

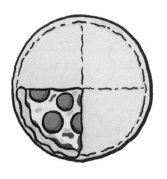 

1. _____ of the pizza was eaten.

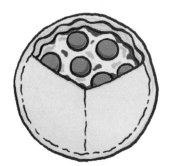  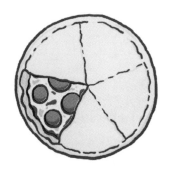

2. _____ of the pizza was eaten.

3. _____ of the pizza was eaten.

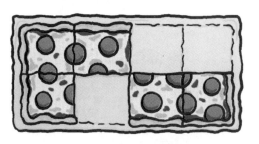 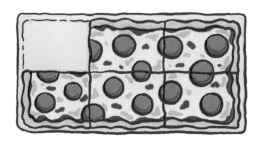

4. _____ of the pizza was eaten.

5. _____ of the pizza was eaten.

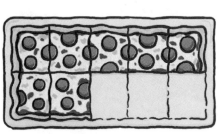 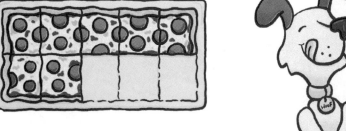 

6. _____ of the pizza was eaten.

7. _____ of the pizza was eaten.

30

ANSWERS

Page 2

Page 5

snake   frog   skunk

flamingo   crocodile   swan

grizzly bear   starfish   crab

Page 9

1. Some kites will not stop crashing!
2. My kite went so high, I could not see it.
3. One kite is not flying.
4. Father says he is glad we came.
5. I did not know kites were so much fun.
6. I can not wait to come back.
7. I will bring a new kite next time.

Pages 12–13

1. northeast
2. southwest
3. Lake Sycamore
4. Sunnyville
5. Lake Sycamore
6. Loon Lake

Page 3

Pages 6–7

1. mammals
2. reptiles
3. birds
4. amphibians
5. insects
6. fish

1   5   4   6

1   5   2   3

Page 10

1. Estimate will vary.   9
2. Estimate will vary.   14
3. Estimate will vary.   22
4. Estimate will vary.   28

Page 14

1. 51   soup
2. 61   pizza
3. 3   milk
4. 58   juice
5. 52   orange
6. 26   apple

Page 4

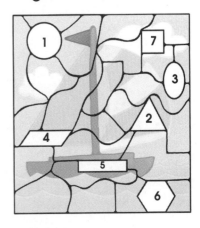

Page 8

Riddle:
A flea market

Page 11

1. A   5. A
2. S   6. A
3. A   7. S
4. S

Page 15

1. boys, girls, grass
2. swings
3. ran
4. blew
5. Noun will vary. N
6. Verb will vary. V
7. Noun will vary. N
8. Verb will vary. V
9. Verb will vary. V

Pages 16–17

1. Dallas
2. north
3. rainy and hot
4. sunny and warm
5. east
6. hail

Page 20

a: now   e: then   f: now

d: then   c: now   b: then

Page 23

1. Fluffy
2. Shelley
3. Buster
4. Posey
5. Squawk

Page 27

1. 1 quarter, 2 dimes, 2 pennies
2. 3 quarters, 1 dime, 1 nickel, 4 pennies
3. 4 quarters, 2 pennies
4. 2 quarters, 2 dimes, 1 penny

Try It!
53¢

Page 28

1. 3 1 4 2
2. 1 4 2 3
3. 2 3 4 1

Page 18

	1	2	3	4	5	6	7
football							
swimming							
soccer							
baseball							
running							
skating							

1. 4
2. 1
3. 21

Page 21

1. 24
2. 11
3. 8
4. $0.30
5. 96

Page 22

1. My best friend will visit on saturday. **Saturday**
2. His name is tom lee. **Tom Lee**
3. He lives on south street. **South Street**
4. Tom's birthday is in march. **March**
5. We go to parkside school. **Parkside School**
6. Our teacher is mrs. montez. **Mrs. Montez**

Pages 24–25

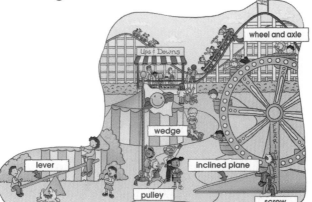

wheel and axle, wedge, inclined plane, lever, pulley, screw

Page 26

Page 19

1. 3
2. 4
3. 5
4. 4
5. 4

Cool Idea
May 10, 2002
July 31, 2003
September 23, 2002

Page 29

1. 4 hundreds + 3 tens + 6 ones
   4 3 6 = 400 + 30 + 6
2. 6 hundreds + 1 ten + 3 ones
   6 1 3 = 600 + 10 + 3
3. 8 hundreds + 0 tens + 4 ones
   8 0 4 = 800 + 0 + 4
4. 2 hundreds + 7 tens + 7 ones
   2 7 7 = 200 + 70 + 7
5. 4 hundreds + 8 tens + 0 ones
   4 8 0 = 400 + 80 + 0

Page 30

1. 3/4
2. 2/3
3. 4/5
4. 3/8
5. 1/6
6. 3/10
7. 5/8